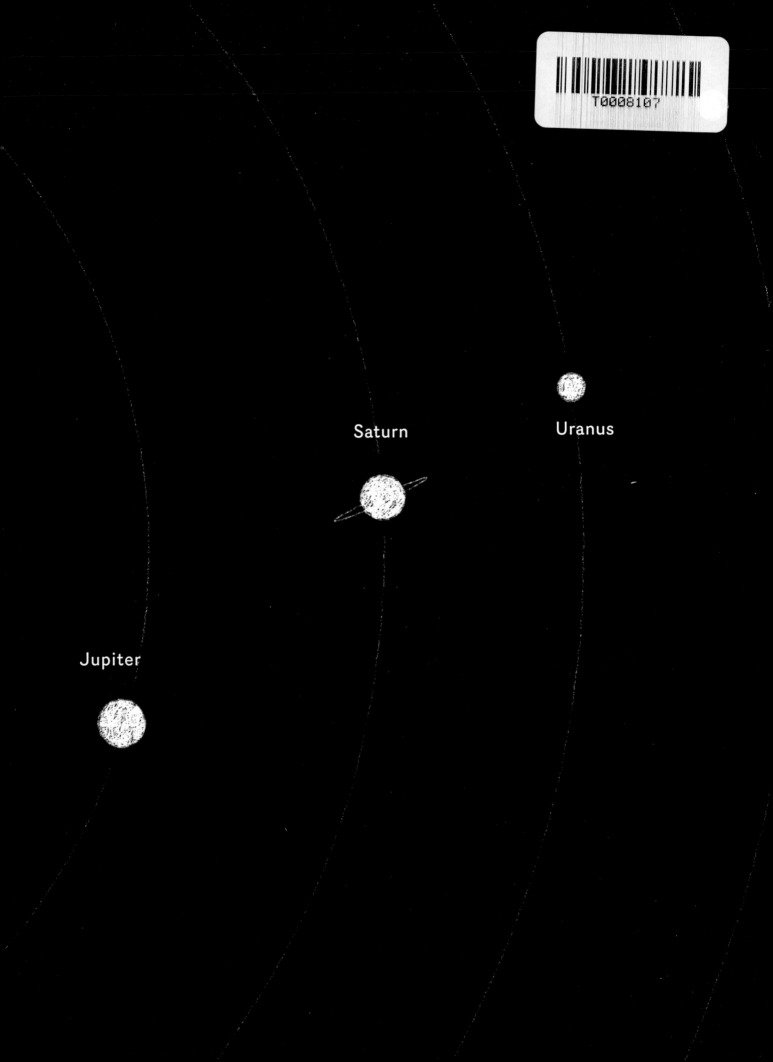

JÉRÉMIE DECALF is a French illustrator and photographer based in San Francisco. Since his childhood, he has been fascinated by space exploration, including the *Voyager* probes and their discoveries. *The Sky Is Not the Limit* has been translated into Korean, Spanish, and Italian, and is Jérémie's English-language debut. Follow Jérémie on Instagram @lomki and visit his website at lomki.com.

First published in the United States in 2023
by Eerdmans Books for Young Readers,
an imprint of Wm. B. Eerdmans Publishing Co.
Grand Rapids, Michigan

www.eerdmans.com/youngreaders

Text and illustrations © 2020 Jérémie Decalf

Originally published in France as *La Nuit est pleine de promesses*
© 2020 Éditions Amaterra, Lyon, France

English-language translation © 2023 Jérémie Decalf
English translation rights arranged through Ttipi Agency, Nantes, France

Manufactured in Canada

31 30 29 28 27 26 25 24 23   1 2 3 4 5 6 7 8 9

ISBN 978-0-8028-5602-9

A catalog record of this book is available from the Library of Congress.

Illustrations created digitally.

JÉRÉMIE DECALF

THE SKY IS NOT THE LIMIT

EERDMANS BOOKS FOR YOUNG READERS

GRAND RAPIDS, MICHIGAN

Since the dawn of time,
we have raised our heads
and wondered . . .

What is up there?

I was built so that we
could find out a little more.

Once finished,
I was loaded onto a rocket.

It is time. I am leaving.

I rise up.
I am above the clouds.
I cross through the daylight.

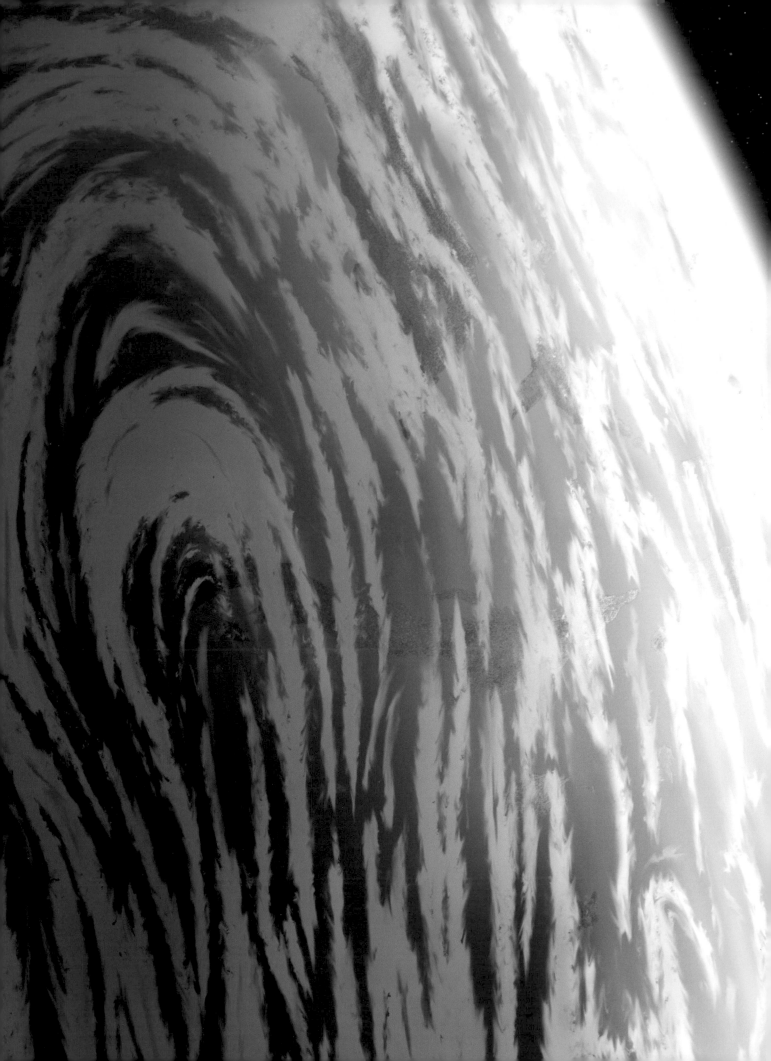

I liberate myself.
Behind me, Earth.

Ahead of me lies the night.

Deep.
Infinite.

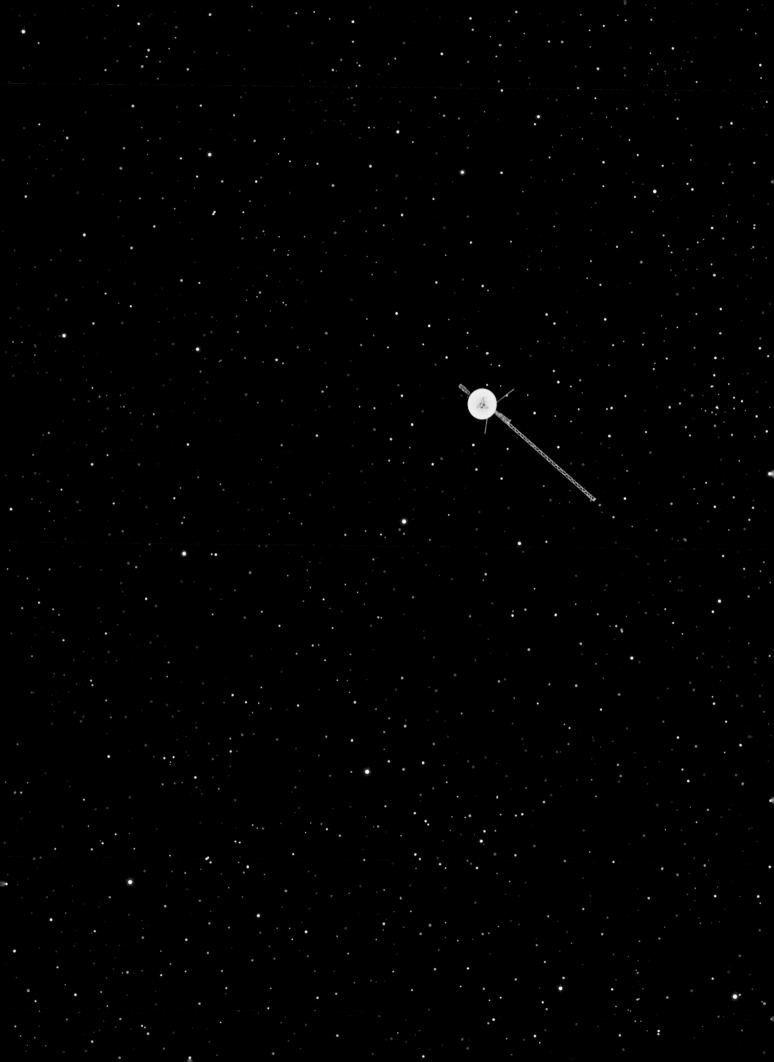

Months—years.

Miles of emptiness.
Some rocks.

And suddenly . . .

Jupiter.

Barely time for a glance.
Nothing stops my advance.

Space.

Neither up,

nor down.

Wonders abound.

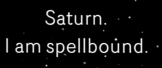

Saturn.
I am spellbound.

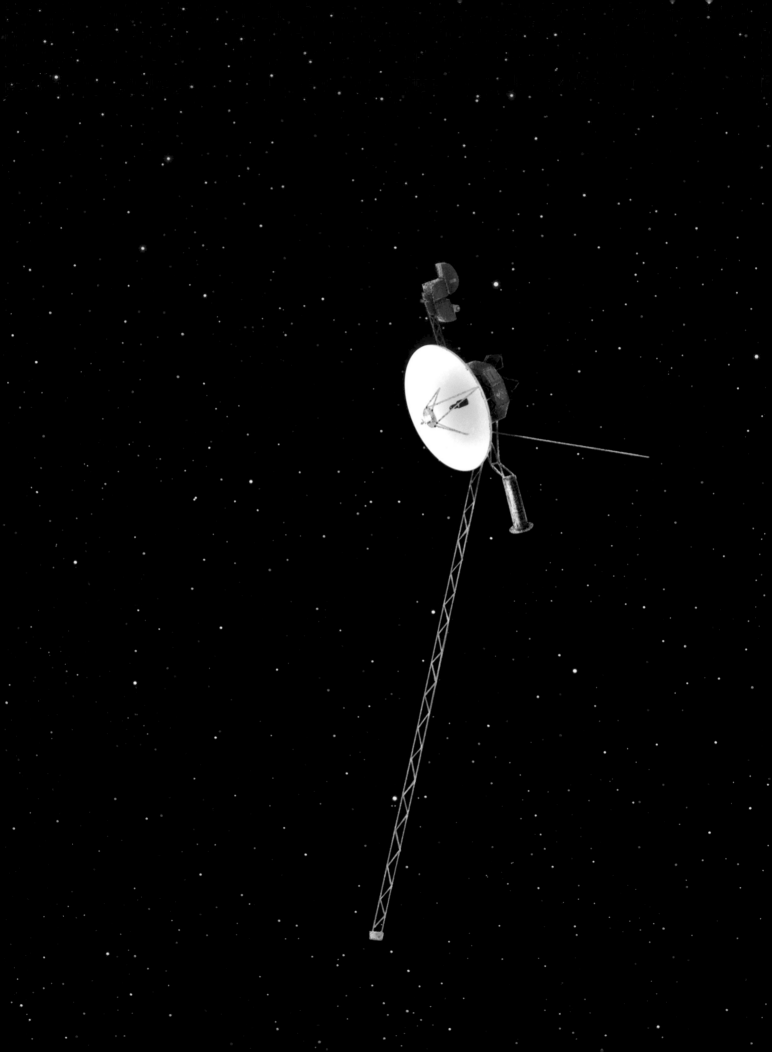

Earth is nowhere to be seen.

But the blue of Uranus . . .

...and farther away, the blue of Neptune—
remind me of where I come from.

And then?

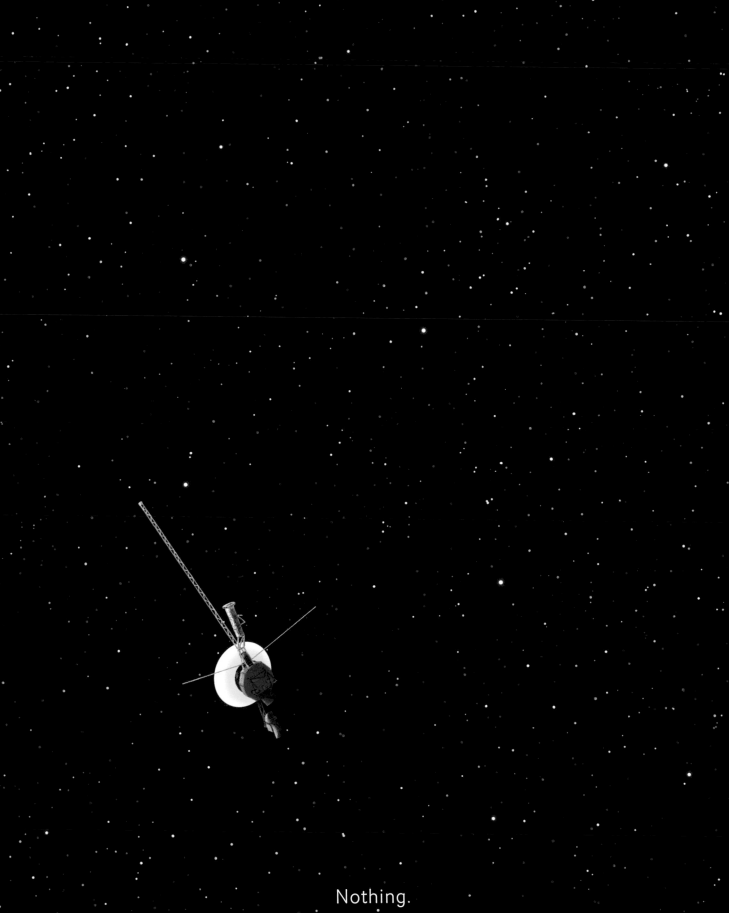

Nothing.

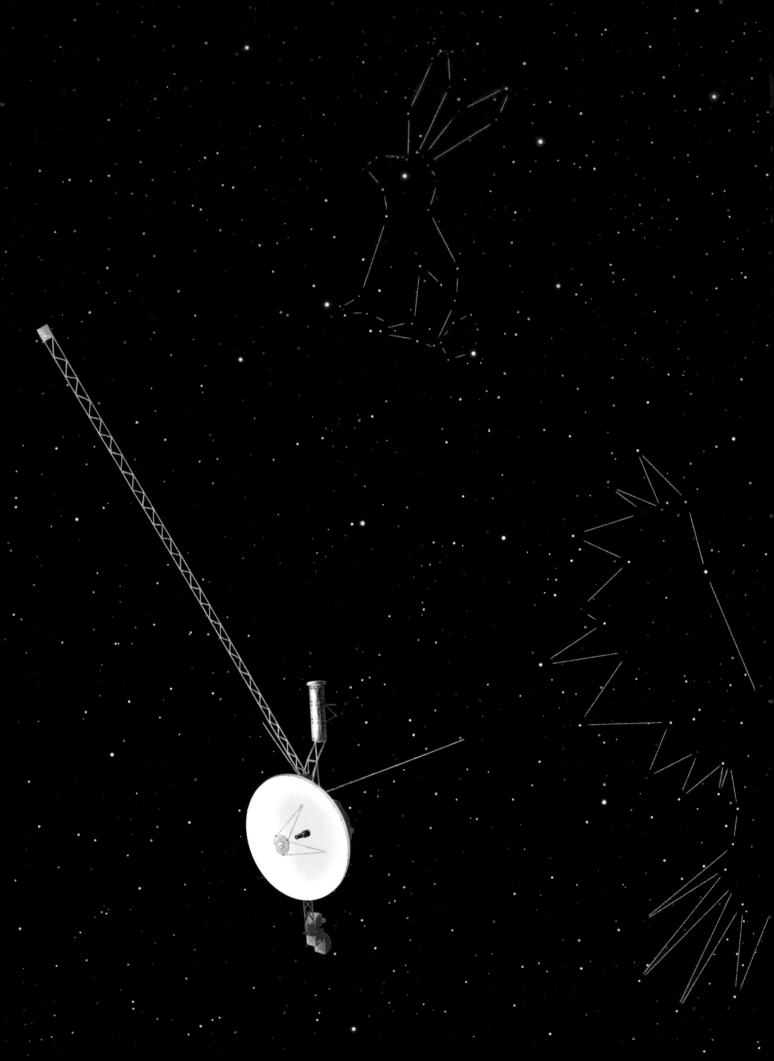

The sun has become just another star,
and my imagination wanders far.

There is a Golden Record on my side.
It is a message,
a bottle sent out to sea.
With images from Earth, and some melodies.

For an encounter, perhaps,
at the edge of night.

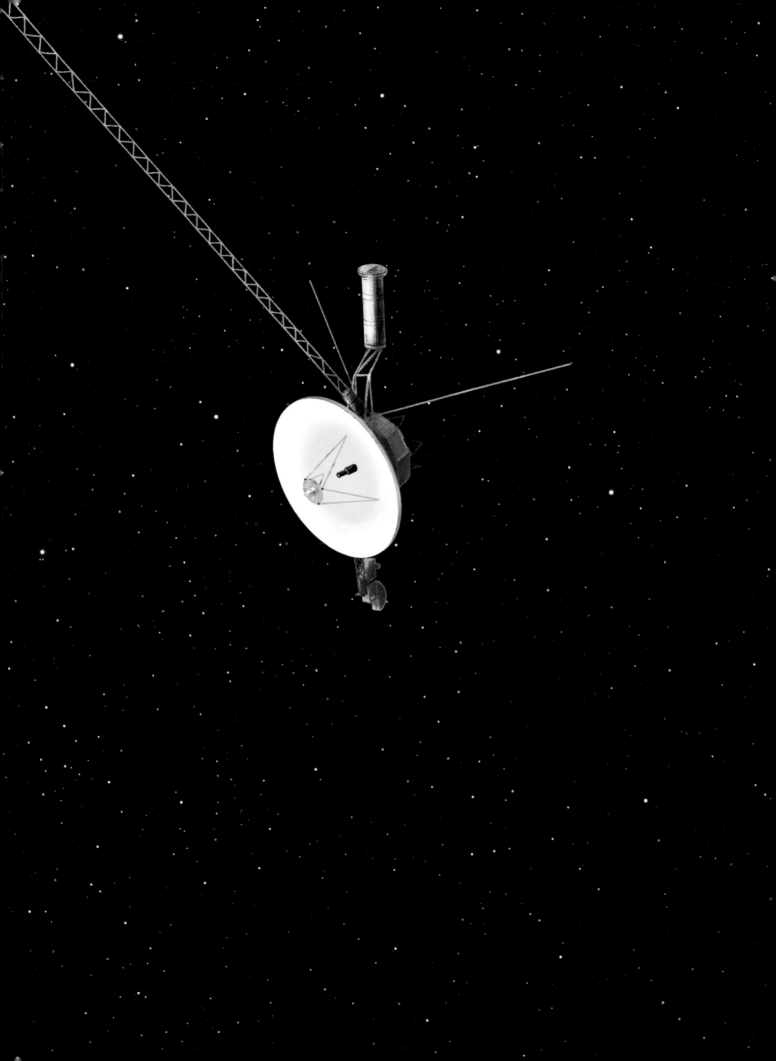

With some new friends?

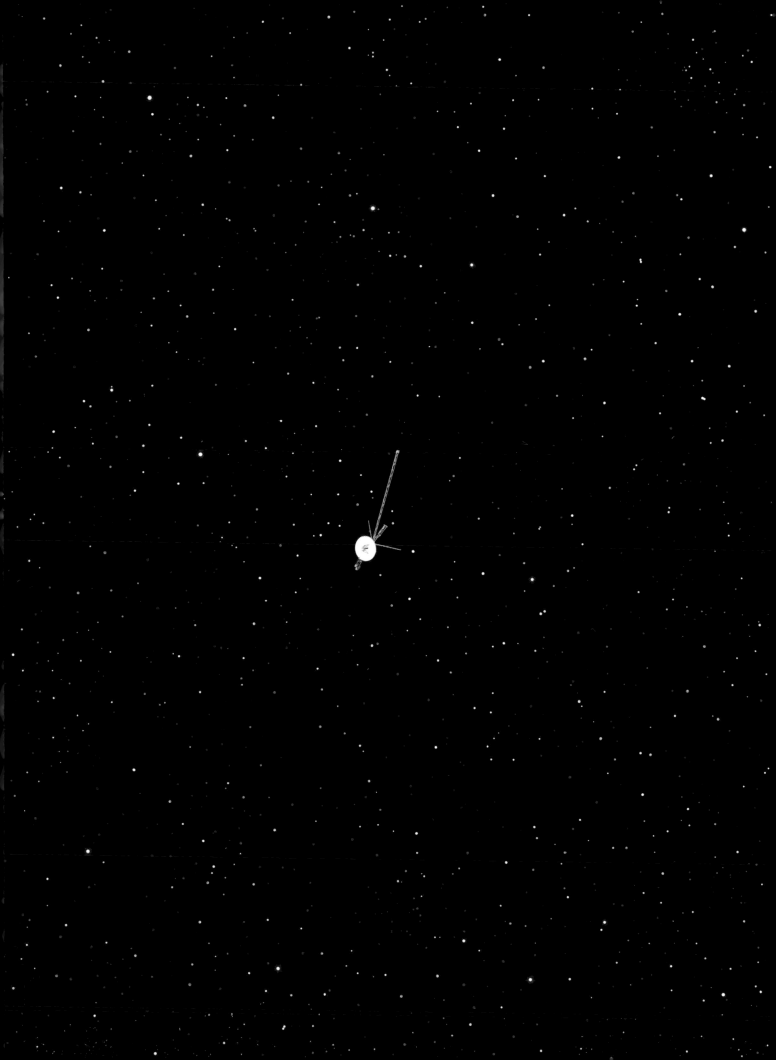

If you look up at the stars
on a summery night . . .

...think of me, out there...

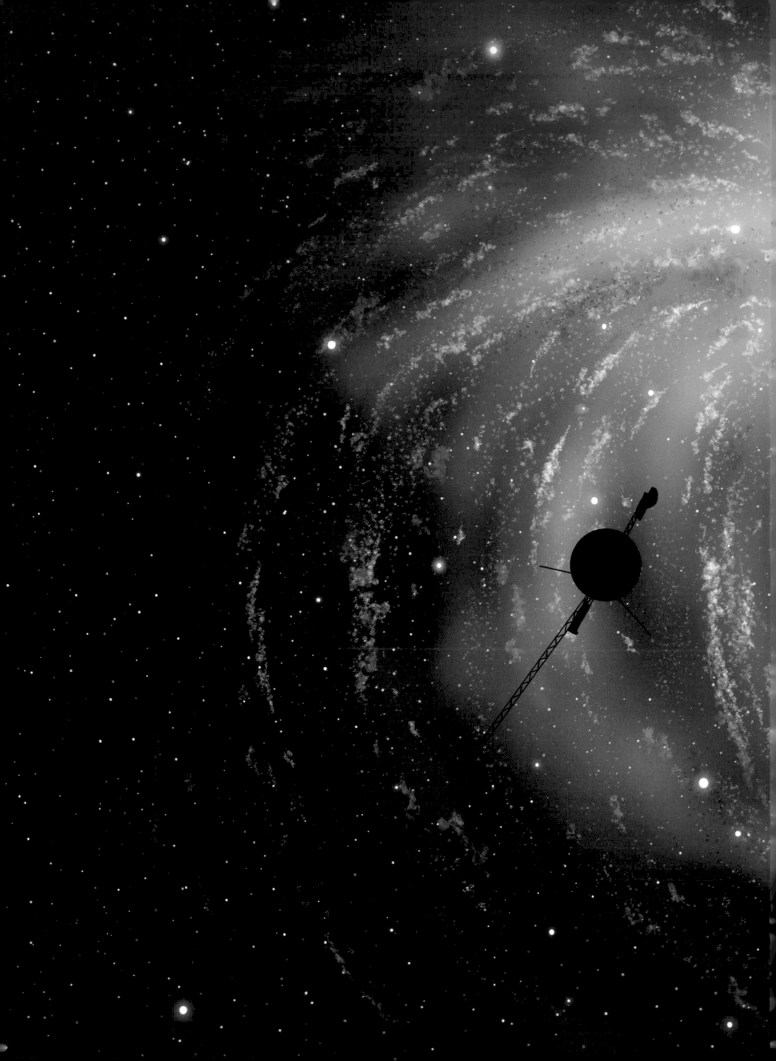

. . . as I continue my voyage.

Launched by NASA during the summer of 1977, *Voyager 2* and its *Voyager 1* twin were among the first spacecraft to reach Jupiter and Saturn. The probes captured the first close-up photos of Jupiter's and Saturn's moons, revealing colorful surfaces, active volcanoes, and freezing cold geysers. Then the spacecraft siblings separated. *Voyager 1* headed toward interstellar space, while *Voyager 2* pushed toward Uranus and Neptune. In 1986 *Voyager 2* became the first human-made object to fly past Uranus, discovering ten new moons and two new rings. Three years later, the probe made history again as the first human-made object to fly by Neptune. There it found five new moons, four new rings, and a "Great Dark Spot" (a huge spinning storm around the size of planet Earth).

In its first few decades, the *Voyager* mission had made incredible scientific discoveries and helped us learn about the striking beauty of our spatial neighborhood. But after *Voyager 2*'s trip to Neptune, it was time to head farther away from home. In 2012 *Voyager 1* flew past the outermost atmosphere of our sun and into interstellar space—becoming the first spacecraft to ever travel that far from Earth. In 2018 *Voyager 2* joined its sibling in that historic territory, becoming the second-ever human-made object in interstellar space. Today, as these probes send back data, they help us learn about the composition of the unexplored places beyond the borders of our solar system.

Both *Voyager* twins carry a copy of the Golden Record, a gold-plated copper disk engraved with information on Earth and its inhabitants. It is a message from humanity to any extraterrestrial civilization that the *Voyager* probes might meet in outer space. The Golden Record's contents reflect life on our planet: images of activities like eating, running, and reading; natural sounds like thunder, laughter, and birds; and greetings in ancient and modern languages like Urdu, Polish, and Quechua. The Golden Record also includes ninety minutes of global and historical music: from a Bach concerto to a Peruvian wedding song, from Chuck Berry's guitar to Kesarbai Kerkar's performance of "Jaat Kahan Ho."

In 2022 NASA started to turn off some of the *Voyager* probes' systems, marking the beginning of the end of their mission. Scientists expect the spacecraft's electricity to last until about 2030. But even when all their instruments have lost power, and none of their data can be sent back to Earth, the *Voyager* twins will keep traveling past the stars, carrying Golden Records for anyone longing to learn more about faraway planet Earth.

Learn more about the *Voyager* mission, view photos captured by *Voyager 1* and *Voyager 2*, and find news updates on the probes' journey at voyager.jpl.nasa.gov.

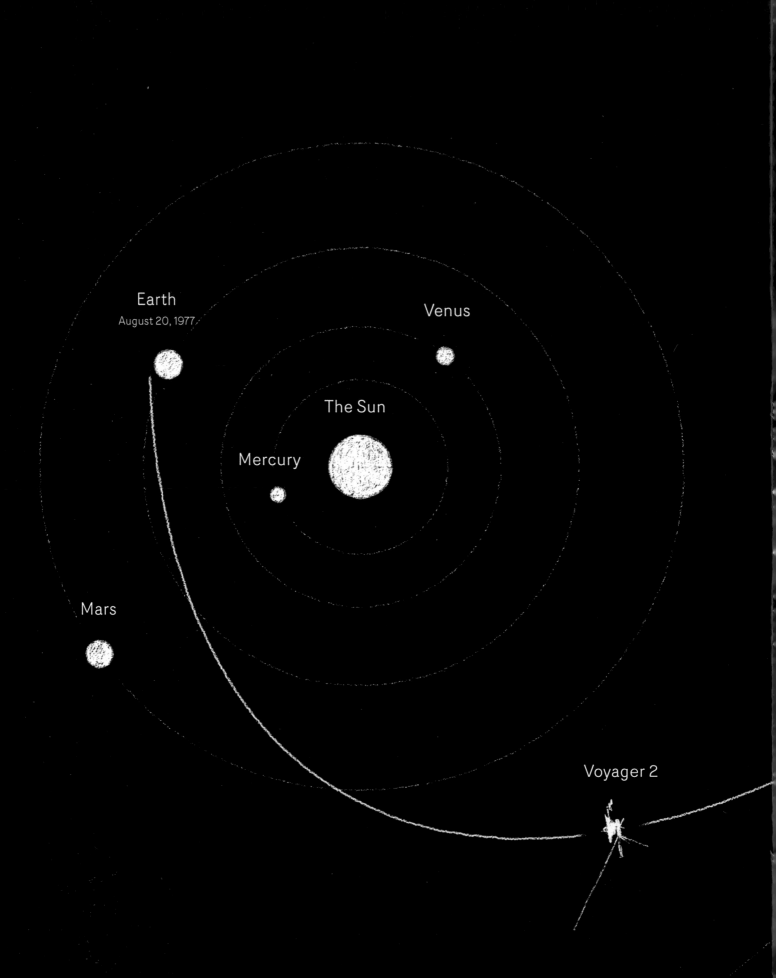

Earth
August 20, 1977

Venus

The Sun

Mercury

Mars

Voyager 2